THE SECOND WORLD WAR IN PHOTOGRAPHS

1943

JOHN CHRISTOPHER & CAMPBELL McCUTCHEON

AMBERLEY

First published 2015

Amberley Publishing
The Hill, Stroud
Gloucestershire, GL5 4EP

www.amberley-books.com

British Library Cataloguing in Publication Data.
A catalogue record for this book is available from the British Library.

ISBN 978 1 4456 2213 2 (print)
ISBN 978 1 4456 2229 3 (ebook)

Typeset in 11pt on 15pt Sabon.
Typesetting and Origination by Amberley Publishing.
Printed in the UK.

Contents

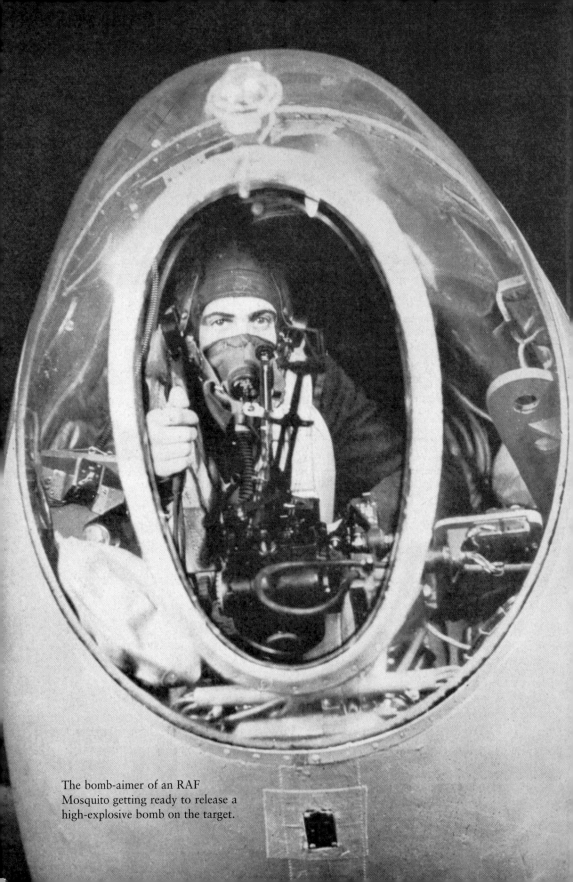

The bomb-aimer of an RAF
Mosquito getting ready to release a
high-explosive bomb on the target.

Introduction: On the Offensive

Three and a half years into the Second World War and, finally, the Allies were on the offensive. The Germans had been halted and defeated at Stalingrad and they would face the world's greatest tank battle at Kursk, where they would suffer huge defeats. In North Africa, Italy and Germany would be thrown off the continent in 1943 and Italy would capitulate after both Sicily and the mainland were invaded by the Allies. Japan had suffered defeats in 1942 that saw her naval strength decimated and, in Burma, the British and Chinese forced the Japanese on to the defensive, as did the Americans in the Solomons and Papua New Guinea. The tide had most definitely turned at last after three years of defeat after defeat for the Allies.

Since August 1942, the Germans and their allies have been trying to invade the Caucasus, hoping to reach the oil-rich areas just beyond, and to conquer the agriculturally rich land too. On 1 January, the Russians begin an offensive in an effort to encircle German troops in the northern Caucasus. The Russian South Front takes the fight towards Rostov and the Germans withdraw over the Terek River on 3 January. On the other side of the world, in the Pacific, the Americans have invaded Buna on 2 January but meet stiff Japanese resistance on the east coast. After copying the idea from the Italians, British navy crews use human torpedoes, or chariots, to attack the Italians in Palermo, Sicily. They sink the cruiser *Ulpio* and a tanker on the third. In the Atlantic, over six days between 3 and 9 January, seven oil tankers in convoy TM-1 heading from the Caribbean to the Mediterranean are sunk by U-boats. Nearly 100,000 tons of valuable fuel and oil are lost. In North Africa, a new army is formed by the US. The 5th Army is commanded by Lt General Mark Clark. From Cape Serrat on the Mediterranean coast to Gafsa, far inland, the Allies sit and wait for Erwin Rommel's Afrika Korps to make their move. Admiral Raeder resigns as head of the German navy after the defeats in the Battle of the Barents Sea in December. He is quickly replaced by Karl Doenitz.

6 January sees the start of the Battle of Huon Gulf, as the Allies launch multiple attacks on Japanese troop convoys heading for Papua New Guinea. Over three days, three transports are sunk and eighty Japanese aircraft are destroyed. The Japanese-controlled Chinese government declares war on the USA and the UK on 9 January. The Russians begin to pick off the Germans in Stalingrad. The 6th Army is trapped there and on 10 January the Russians split them into pockets. In Southern

Russia, the Axis forces are on the defensive. The Japanese feel the same pressure on 10 January, with an onslaught by 50,000 American troops on Guadalcanal, who attempt to destroy the Japanese forces on the island. Some 15,000 Japanese are holed up in the jungle and they are forced back by the end of the month, when the survivors evacuate the island from Tassafaronga Point. In Papua, the Japanese lose control of the Kokoda Trail on 13 January. This vital link to Port Moresby is denied to the Japanese. It has been ten months of hard fighting by the Americans under General MacArthur to turn the tide in Papua New Guinea. Between 14 and 23 January, President Roosevelt and Prime Minister Winston Churchill meet at Casablanca. The discussions show just how far apart the two allies are in their ideas for defeating the Germans and Italians. The British want to invade Europe's soft underbelly, hoping to knock Italy out of the war, while also tying up German troops in the South, helping make their defences in France and the Low Countries weaker. The Americans wanted to go straight for northern France but with no hope of an invasion in 1943, it was decided to attack Sicily once North Africa had been cleared of the enemy. The Allies go on the offensive in Africa on 15 January, with the British attacking Rommel at Buerat, quickly pushing his forces back as far as Homs, only 100 miles from Tripoli. Homs is reached on 19 January and Tripoli is abandoned to conserve Rommel's troops and supplies on 22 January, making a stand near Mareth instead. On 18 January, the Jews revolt in the Warsaw ghetto. Mass deportations to the death camps had taken place in 1942 and the resumption of these triggered the revolt. In Papua New Guinea the Americans capture Sanananda and prepare to take Lae and Salamua. The Japanese will ultimately evacuate Papua, having lost air and sea control around Papua. On 30 January, the British Royal Air Force makes its first daylight raid of the war over Berlin.

Between 1 and 9 February, the Japanese evacuate the remaining 13,000 troops from Guadalcanal. They have lost 10,000 dead to a mere 1,600 for the Americans. It is the first major land defeat for the Japanese in the war. Germany too suffers its most humiliating defeat of the war so far, with the loss of its 6th Army in Stalingrad. Having suffered privations, disease, hunger and the onslaught of the Soviets, Field Marshal von Paulus capitulates. The remaining 93,000 troops trapped in Stalingrad surrender and are marched into captivity. Operation Gondola begins on 4 February. American and British bombers seek out U-boats in the Bay of Biscay, using powerful searchlights and radar to surprise the submarines on the surface at night. Kursk is taken by the Russians on 8 February. It will be the venue for the most spectacular tank battle in history later in the year. The Afrika Korps suffers a setback on 9 February as a convoy of much-needed supplies is intercepted by Allied aircraft from Malta. The bombers sink ten vessels between 9 February and 22 March, severely disrupting German supply routes. Numerous other ships are sunk by mine and British submarines from Gibraltar and Malta. In the Caucasus, the Soviets take Krasnodar on the 12th and capture Rostov on the 14th. The expected offensive by Rommel begins on 14 February. He attacks north-west from Mareth. At the Kasserine Pass, his troops cause chaos in the ranks of the US II Corps. By 22 February, the German offensive has run out of steam at Thala and Rommel orders a withdrawal. The eight days of fighting see 2,000 Germans and Italians lost and 10,000 American troops

Above: 'Taxi to Moscow.' Hitler is at the wheel in this British wartime cartoon by Illingworth.

killed or captured. On 15 February, Kharkov is captured by the Russians. Other towns and cities fall as the Russians conquer lost ground. German students protest against the war and Hitler in Munich and other cities. Two leaders of the White Rose anti-Nazi student group, Hans and Sophie Scholl, are beheaded on 21 February in Munich.

Brigadier Orde Wingate's Chindits begin their 'behind enemy lines' operations on 18 February, as 3,000 men begin their mission to disrupt Japanese supply lines. There is limited military success during the six-week-long mission but it helps tie up many Japanese soldiers. Supplied by air, the Chindits will make more missions throughout the year. Field Marshal von Manstein makes an attack against the Soviets on 18 February in an attempt to stop the enemy offensive around the Dniepr river. Three Soviet armies are surrounded by von Manstein's four panzer corps, which inflict severe casualties on the Russians over nine days. In the North Atlantic, from 20–25 February, convoy ON-166 loses fifteen of forty-nine ships for the loss of a solitary U-boat. The German wolf-packs can still operate with impunity at times. Russell Island, one of the Solomon group, is invaded on 21 February, as a prelude to the conquest of the whole group. It is the beginning of the 'island-hopping' strategy devised by Admiral Chester Nimitz and General Douglas MacArthur. The Americans will bypass certain well-defended islands and starve them of supplies and ammunition, while creeping ever further forward towards mainland Japan. Another wolf pack attacks convoy UC-1 on the night of 23/24 February, sinking seven tankers. On 26–28 February, the Germans make an attack from their lines at Mareth but it is unsuccessful. The month ends with Norwegian paratroops making an attack on the Norsk Hydro power station at Rjukan, Norway. This was the

Above: A British 6-pounder anti-tank gun crew in the hills near Medjez-el-Bab, on the road to Tebourba in northern Africa. *Below:* 'Women of Britain at work.' Two girls at a Government electrical training centre in the north-east of England learning to wire battleships. The course lasted twelve weeks, after which they were assigned to a Tyneside shipyard.

only site in Europe capable of making deuterium oxide, which the Allies feared the Germans could use in their atomic research.

March begins with the Americans and Australians attacking eight Japanese transports and eight destroyers in the Battle of the Bismarck Sea. The Japanese ships are sailing from Rabaul to Lae. US and Australian aircraft sink all but four destroyers. They lose four aircraft while the Japanese suffer twenty-five losses to go with their ships, which are now at the bottom of the ocean. The Japanese fail to reinforce New Guinea and the troops there are now on their own. 367 British aircraft attack the Krupp works at Essen in the Ruhr on 5 March. Fourteen bombers are lost and the raid signals the start of a four-month bomber offensive on Germany's industrial heartland. The Afrika Korps attacks Montgomery's troops in North Africa but are forced back and Rommel, who is suffering under the strain of the desert war, leaves Africa for Europe. More wolf pack attacks take place between 6 and 20 March. The convoys HX-229 and SC-122 are attacked by around twenty U-boats. Twenty-one ships will not reach port and the Germans lose a solitary submarine. This level of losses cannot be sustained.

A bomb is placed aboard Hitler's aircraft by disaffected army officers on 13 March, but it fails to explode. The Soviet 3rd Tank Army is destroyed by Manstein's forces, which reach the Donets River on 14 March. In his campaign, he has captured 6,000 square miles, while his counteroffensive has stabilised the German fronts and removed a whole army that once faced it. The next day, Kharkov is recaptured, with Beograd being taken on 18 March. The end of March sees the Russians thrown back all the way to the Donets River. The Germans begin planning for Operation Citadel, where they intend to capture the Kursk salient and destroy the half a million Russian soldiers in Kursk and to the west. In the meantime, the German advance halts as the spring thaw begins. March is the month for major offensives and another begins on the Mareth Line in Tunisia on 20 March. It will continue for eight days. Montgomery's troops penetrate the line along the banks of the Wadi Zigzaou between 21 and 22 March. The German 15th Panzer Division counterattacks successfully but, by 26 March, the Axis forces are on the turn and have retreated to the El Hamma plain. The Germans retreat to Wadi Akarit on 28 March but many of the Italian soldiers simply give up and surrender. In the Bering Sea, a force of four Japanese cruisers and five destroyers clashes with two American cruisers and four destroyers in the Battle of the Kommandorsky Islands on 26 March. The Japanese abandon the action after they have a cruiser badly damaged, but just before they can use their numerical superiority to win the battle. The Americans have a cruiser damaged too. The Germans have reinforced their naval forces in Norway and the British suspend convoys to Russia via the North Cape at the end of March as the daylight hours are extended. They simply cannot guarantee the safety of the ships due to German naval and air forces in the area.

April sees the British 8th Army, the Desert Rats, attack the Wadi Akarit line on the 5th. This defensive position cannot be bypassed and has to be taken straight on. The attack is successful but the British do not exploit their good fortune, giving the Axis forces time to regroup and dig in. The next Allied target in Tunisia is the

Foundouk Pass, which is attacked on 7 April. Between then and the tenth, the Axis forces fight a spirited rearguard action, enabling them to withdraw most of their troops. In the Pacific, 180 Japanese aircraft attack Allied shipping off Guadalcanal, signaling the start of Operation I. On 11 April, the Japanese attack New Guinea and ships off the coast, as well as Port Moresby airfield on 12 April. The British are attacked at Milne Bay on the 13th. The aerial battle against Allied shipping sees the loss of a destroyer, one corvette, a tanker, two cargo ships and twenty Allied aircraft but the aerial operation does not have the success the Japanese hope for. British troops enter Sfax on 10 April, quickly bringing the port back into action and shortening the supply lines for the Allied offensive. The Axis forces, however, have lost their main ports of supply, and Allied air superiority means their forces cannot easily be supplied by air. Their defeat is inevitable but they must hold on until such time as they can delay the potential invasion of Italy until the autumn, when the weather will turn for the worse and make Allied landings more difficult. On 12 April, in Poland, the Germans announce the discovery of a mass grave in the Katyn forest. The bodies represent many Polish soldiers, mainly officers, killed by the Russians in 1939 after the invasion of the country. On 17 April, the American 8th Army Air Force launches raids on Bremen and its aircraft factories. Sixteen of the 115 B-17 Flying Fortresses are lost.

The Americans shoot down around half of 100 German transport aircraft and ten fighter escorts, which are trying to supply Axis forces in Tunisia from the air. The next day, on 19 April, Montgomery launches an offensive against Enfidaville but the

On 22 September 1943, the German battleship *Tirpitz* was attacked by a group of British X-craft midget submarines, but it wouldn't be until the following year that she was finally sunk in an air strike, shown left.

attack is quickly bogged down and casualties are high. The Final Solution is enacted in Warsaw, when SS troops enter the ghetto there and begin to clear it. Around 310,000 Jews have already been deported to death camps and those that remain have acquired weapons and have had time to create tunnels and defences within the ghetto. They know they will die and will die fighting rather than be herded into gas chambers. British and American soldiers prepare to attack the strongpoints spread in front of Tunis on 22 April. By 26 April, the British 1st Army's V Corps has taken Longstop Hill and is in front of Djebel Bou Aoukaz. The US II Corps takes Hill 609 but its progress is blocked by strong German defences. Montgomery sends two divisions and a brigade to help the Americans. The month ends with two rather different submarine actions. On 28 April, the convoy ONS-5 is attacked by fifty-one U-boats and in a running seven-day battle, seven U-boats are sunk, with seventeen damaged, for the loss of thirteen of forty-two ships. Meanwhile, Operation Mincemeat was launched on 30 April. A body, dressed as a British officer, is dumped from a submarine off the coast of Spain. Attached to the body is a briefcase full of documents suggesting the Allies will attack Greece and Sardinia and not Sicily after they have conquered North Africa. The Germans are informed of the find by the Spanish and copy the documents. They fall hook, line and sinker for the deception and swiftly move reinforcements to Greece and Sardinia.

In Tunisia, Djebel Bou Aoukaz is captured on 5 May by the 8th and 1st Armies. This lets the 7th Armoured Division head into open country, where they can use their tanks to overcome the weaker German and Italian forces. Advance is rapid and Massicault is reached on 6 May, with the outskirts of Tunis the next day. Bizerta is reached the same day by the Americans. The days of Axis rule in North Africa are almost over and the enemy have no means of escape. Attu Island is attacked on 11 May by 12,000 US soldiers. The fighting does not cease until 29 May, by which time virtually all of the island's 2,500 Japanese soldiers are killed. Only twenty-nine survive the onslaught with the Americans losing 561 dead and 1,136 wounded. Another conference is held between Roosevelt and Churchill, this time in Washington. The Trident Conference between 12 and 25 May sets the scene for the rest of 1943 and 1944, with a provisional date of 1 May 1944 set for the invasion of northern France. The British demand that mainland Italy is invaded as well as Sicily. The two allies agree that bombing raids across Europe are intensified. Soon the Allies will have the ability to bomb Europe flying from North Africa too. On the second day of the conference, Axis forces in Tunisia surrender and some 620,000 Germans and Italians are captured, wounded or killed over the campaign for the loss of 20,000 French, 19,000 British and 18,500 Americans. North Africa is now free. Another success in the month is the daring raid by 617 Squadron on the night of 16/17 May. Nineteen specially modified Lancasters attack numerous dams on the Mohne and Eder rivers, destroying two and damaging another. Eight Lancasters are lost but they have left many parts of the Ruhr under water. The Warsaw Ghetto uprising comes to an end on 16 May, with the Germans having killed 14,000 and sent another 22,000 to their deaths, with 20,000 Jews forced into labour camps, where many will die too.

In a total reverse of fortunes from earlier in the year, Admiral Doenitz withdraws his submarines from parts of the North Atlantic on 22 May, having lost fifty-six U-boats to the Allies in the previous six weeks. The loss of valuable crews and submarines cannot be sustained. Dortmund is attacked on 23 May by hundreds of British heavy bombers. Wuppertal is attacked on the 29th and 2,450 are killed under the hail of bombs. On 26 May, the Axis forces are thrown at around 16,000 Communist partisans in Montenegro, in Yugoslavia. The Allies are supplying the rebels with tons of equipment, arms and ammunition.

Between 1 and 11 June, Pantelleria island, off Italy, is pummelled by aircraft and ships and the supposedly impregnable island is forced to surrender on 11 June. It is the last major obstacle in the way of the invasion of Sicily. On 10 June, Operation Point Blank begins. This is one of the outcomes of the Washington Trident Conference and will lead the bombing by day and by night of Germany that will not stop until the invasion of France in 1944. The British spend the nights saturation bombing both civilian and military targets, while the Americans spend their days precision bombing German aircraft factories and suppliers. Britain's RAF introduces a Pathfinder system, using highly skilled crews to mark the targets for the carpet-bombing that will follow. Between 20 and 24 June, the first shuttle raid takes place between North Africa and Britain. The first flights fly from East Coast airfields for Friedrichshafen and fly on to Africa, then return, attacking La Spezia, before overflying France and Germany to return back home. In the Pacific, the Solomons see an offensive by the US against the New Georgia island group. Munda airfield is attacked and is the major objective. The US Navy shells the islands and also mines the surrounding seas to prevent resupply.

The Polish president in exile, Wladyslaw Raczkiewcz, is killed in a plane crash on 5 July. US troops land on New Georgia on 5 July and that evening a Japanese destroyer is sunk off Kola Gulf. The Soviets discover German plans for an assault at Kursk, using 900,000 troops and thousands of tanks. The build-up had taken place from March. The Russians try and beat the Germans down by bombarding them before the assault. They have gathered 1.3 million soldiers to face the Germans. Operation Citadel begins on 6 July with the Germans attacking the salient west of Kharkov. The Ninth Army manages six miles for the cost of 250,000 men. Some 6,000 tanks and guns face each other in the world's biggest ever tank battle. The Germans push thousands of more men into the assault but the Russians contain them. The Russians have superiority in the air and huge lines of defences and this means the Germans cannot push through their lines.

The Australians capture Mumbo, a Japanese stronghold in Papua New Guinea, on 7 July, while US and Australian forces try and dislodge the retreating Japanese from their new defences. More troops are landed to dislodge the Japanese from Papua. On 9 July, Sicily is attacked from the air, with British and American airborne landings on the island. Air bases on Sardinia, Sicily and mainland Italy have already been pummelled by bombers. The Italians expect the main attack to be in Sardinia and are caught by surprise by the attack on Sicily. The Allies hope to pull troops from the Eastern Front, helping the Russians, clear the Mediterranean for their own ships, opening up a short route for convoys via the Suez Canal, rather than via South Africa, and speed up the capitulation of Italy. On 10 July, 2,500 ships of all sizes appear off the coast of Sicily and the invasion proper begins. The weather is stormy and the Italians do not expect the Allies to attempt a landing in such weather. There are 230,000 Italian troops in Sicily, as well as 40,000 Germans, who will ultimately face 160,000 Allied troops from the British 8th Army and the US 7th Army. For the first time in action, a new weapon is used, the amphibious truck known as a DUKW.

The German Hermann Göring Panzer Division counter-attacks in Sicily on 11 July, but is held up by paratroops near Gela and Licata and cannot engage. The British 8th Army advances up the coast towards bases at Catania and Messina, the main ferry port back to mainland Italy. As the Allies move through Sicily, the Russians counterattack on the Eastern Front, in the Ukraine. At Kursk, the tank battle to end all tank battles begins. The Germans under von Manstein advance twenty-five miles at a cost of 350 tanks and 10,000 men. To the north, the Soviets attack near Orel. On 13 July, Hitler calls off Citadel and the losses are 550 tanks and half a million men. It is the last major German offensive in the east, and their reserves have been destroyed or severely damaged. In the Pacific, the Japanese sink an American destroyer and damage three cruisers, one from New Zealand, for the loss of one cruiser in the Battle of Kolombangara.

In Sicily, the US Seventh Army pushes for Palermo, capturing the Sicilian capital on 23 July, after an eight-day fight. By 17 July, the Germans in the Ukraine are on the retreat and are hotly pursued by the Russians. Between 17 and 18 July, the 8th Army attacks Catania, but is held back by the Hermann Göring Division, and as a result they bypass the city. Hitler and Mussolini meet on 19 July in northern Italy. Mussolini endorses Hitler's proposal that the Germans take military control of Italy. That day, US bombers attack Rome. Palermo is captured on 23 July by the American Seventh Army. Trapani and Marsala fall too. By 24 July, the Germans have fallen back to the lines they held before Operation Citadel started. In Sicily, the Allies push on to Messina, with a spirited German defence around Catania and the airfields required to supply their troops in Sicily. For four nights between 24 July and 2 August, huge night-time raids are made on Hamburg. Around 50,000 die and 800,000 are made homeless as the British use foil strips called 'window' to confuse German radar. A firestorm burns Hamburg on the night of 27/28 July. Italy is beginning to fall apart and, on 25 July, Mussolini is relieved of his power and arrested. A new government is formed but it lasts a mere six weeks. The only thing stopping Germany taking control of Italy is the country promising to fight on. Even the Italian government hopes for an Allied invasion to prevent occupation of the country by the Germans. In the Ukraine, the Germans retreat from Orel to the Hagen Line, a hastily prepared defensive line.

1 August sees 178 American bombers fly from Libya to Ploesti, Romania, some 1,000 miles, to bomb the oil fields, which provide most of the oil needs of the Axis. Fifty-four aircraft are damaged after encountering heavy anti-aircraft fire but the raid convinces Hitler that Ploesti is more vulnerable than it really is. With fears of

a Russian summer offensive, Hitler orders von Manstein to hold the area around Kharkov. He does not want the Russians to progress westwards but his armies lack the manpower, tanks and equipment to hold them back for long. Italy sends an intimation that it will sue for peace on 3 August. The Allies agree but under certain conditions, namely that Italian territory can be used to wage war against the Germans, the Italian fleet is to be handed to the Allies and that Allied prisoners in Italy be freed and not be allowed to fall into the hands of the Germans. Between 3 and 16 August, the Italians withdraw from Sicily. Catania is surrendered on 5 August. On the same day, Orel and Belgorod are captured by the Russians. Kharkov will be next. Munda airfield, on the Solomons, is captured and the Japanese defenders of the island of New Georgia are left on their own, with no hope of supply or reinforcement. By 22 August, they are evacuated to nearby Kolombangara.

With Italy in danger of surrendering, Hitler sends huge numbers of soldiers to attempt to take over as much control of the country as possible, to capture the Italian fleet and to rescue Mussolini from imprisonment. The Japanese try and reinforce Kolombangara using four destroyers but on the night of 6/7 August, six American destroyers sink three of the four destroyers, with the loss of 1,210 lives. The American ships are undamaged. The Germans are putting up stubborn resistance in Sicily and the Allies make further landings on the coast near San Stefano. The Germans begin to evacuate by 11 August, with some 100,000 troops withdrawn before Messina falls on the 17th. Casualties are high with around 10,000 Germans killed or captured, 132,000 Italians, most of who have surrendered and the Allies suffer 7,000 deaths and 15,000 injured. Sicily will provide the launch pad for the next stage of the freeing of Europe, the invasion of Italy itself.

Roosevelt and Churchill meet in Quebec, fresh from the success of the invasion of Sicily, to discuss the progress of the war and its next stages. The Americans retain overall control in the Pacific, Chindit operations will continue, as will aid to the Chinese nationalist leader Chiang Kai-shek. The war will continue on the Italian mainland, to capitalise on the overthrow of Mussolini, and the basic plan for Operation Overlord, the invasion of France, is approved and planning begins in earnest for the greatest seaborne invasion of all time. The order is given to construct the huge, floating harbours that will be required. These Mulberry harbours will be built on the Thames and other estuaries and towed to France immediately after D-Day.

Kiska island, in the Pacific, is invaded by a joint American and Canadian force on 15 August but the troops discover the island abandoned and the Japanese garrison already evacuated. Peenemünde, a remote spot in the Baltic, is bombed by 597 British bombers on the night of 16/17 August. The British know of German rocket development and the raid is seen as a means of destroying research, as well as the factory making V1 and V2 rockets. Around 732 die in Peenemünde and the British lose forty bombers. At the same time, the Americans are bombing Schweinfurt and Regensburg in an effort to destroy ball-bearing factories. Fifty of the 230 bombers are lost. Mount Tabu is finally taken on 19 August. In Papua, the Japanese are now sandwiched between the Francisco River and Salamaua. More bad news for the

Axis on 22–23 August, when Kharkov is retaken. The Germans are in trouble in the south of Russia, having lost Kursk, Orel and Kharkov and having seen their reserves wiped out and their armies exhausted. The Russian offensive begins on 26 August, as the Soviets push towards and cross the Dniepr River, which is one of the Germans' main lines of defence in the Ukraine. The Danish government resigns on 28 August as it refuses to collaborate with the Germans. Many of its ships are scuttled or sailed to Sweden to avoid capture by the Germans.

The invasion of Italy begins on 3 September, with a bridgehead being created in Calabria. There is almost no resistance as the Germans in the south of Italy have already begun to withdraw to positions much further north. The day after, the Americans attack Lae, on Papua, hoping to capture the airfield and town. Amphibious landings take place on the 4th, and paratroopers land on the 5th. Italy officially surrenders on the 8th. The Germans take control of much of the north, but the navy manages to get twenty-four vessels to safety in Malta. Allied troops land at the Gulf of Salerno on 9 September. They comprise the US 5th Army and the British X Corps. On the night of 10/11 September, the Germans evacuate 25,000 troops from Sardinia to bolster the defences of northern Italy. In Papua, Salamaua is captured on the 11th, with Lae falling to the Allies four days later. The Japanese still hold a fort at Finschhafen, which needs to be captured so that the sea lanes to New Britain are cleared. This is the next place to be attacked. Mussolini is rescued on 12 September in a daring raid by Otto Skorzeny's commando troops but he is now no more than a puppet of the German regime. The Germans attack at Salerno, threatening the bridgehead. Only huge bombardments from the sea and air save the Allies from being pushed back into the sea. On 15 September, another invasion takes place, this time by British troops on the Aegean island of Kos. The British hope that the island will give easier access to the oilfields at Ploesti, as well as encourage Turkey to enter the war on the side of the Allies. The Germans are in strength around Rhodes and Kos is to be a springboard for an attack against Rhodes. Many of the islands have Italian troops on them and they soon link up with the British. Bryansk is captured on 17 September by the Russians. After a few months, U-boats return to the Atlantic in mid-September. They have been kitted out with radar, anti-aircraft guns and acoustic torpedoes, and are much better prepared for attacks from aircraft and convoy escorts. Twenty U-boats, operating as wolf packs, attack convoys ON-202 and ONS-28 between 18 and 23 September, sinking many warships and cargo vessels. A daring raid by Australian commandos, who have canoed into the harbour of Singapore, sees two Japanese transports sunk on 21 September. In the Crimea, on 22 September, bridgeheads are made across the Dniepr River south of Kiev. In Papua, the Americans land at the Huon Peninsula as they continue the conquest of Papua New Guinea. British midget submarines cripple the *Tirpitz*, which has resolutely remained in Norway, holding up many British warships, which have to contain her in case she breaks out into the open sea. Convoys to Murmansk and Archangel are also threatened by the *Tirpitz*. All three submarines are sunk.

On the night of 22/23 September, Bari is invaded by the British, who advance onwards to Foggia, which is captured, along with its airfield, on 28 September.

On the 23rd, Mussolini announces the creation of the Italian Social Republic. It controls much of north-west Italy but the Germans are given control of other parts of the country. Smolensk is recaptured by the Soviets on 25 September and the Germans are in retreat in the centre of Russia.

Naples is entered by British troops on 1 October, while the US 5th Army advances to the Volturno River, by the 8th. The Germans have blown all of the bridges across and the advance is halted. At Termoli, on the 2nd, British commandos land and are followed by a main force the next day. The Germans attack but they cannot stop the British forces and the town is taken over by 11 October. On the night of 3/4 October, around 1,200 German paratroops land on Kos, capturing 900 Allied and 3,000 Italian troops. They shoot ninety Italian officers for fighting against the Germans. More action in the Aegean as a German convoy heading for Leros is attacked by the Royal Navy on 6 October. Two British cruisers and two destroyers sink seven German transports and their escort. By the 9th, the Caucasus is free of the Nazis as the Soviet army reaches the Kerch Strait. This success is followed by the expansion of the Dniepr bridgehead from 10–20 October. By the 23rd, Zaporoshye and Melitopol are taken from the Germans. The weather has deteriorated in Italy and the Americans make slow progress over the Volturno River. The Italian government, which is strong in southern Italy, declares war on its former ally on 13 October. The Italians have changed side and are now fighting the Germans. A disastrous daytime raid on Schweinfurt takes place on 14 October. The Americans lose sixty of 291 aircraft and another 140 are damaged. This is the last unescorted raid for the US 8th Army Air Force, and long-range fighter escorts will be used from now on. The Allies meet in Moscow on 19 October, and agree the treatment of war criminals at the war's end, the setting up of groups to discuss fate of Italy and the occupied countries of Europe, as well as that of China, postwar. By 22 October, the British 8th Army crosses the Trigno River. The Gustav Line uses the Garigliano and Sangro rivers as part of its defences. Captive Allied slave labour finishes the Burma railway, which connects northern Burma with Siam. Many thousands of both prisoners and local forced labour have died during the construction of the route. Over 12,000 Allied troops have died. October ends with an invasion of the Treasury Islands by US and New Zealand troops. This is a diversionary attack for the main thrust against Bougainville and the Japanese reinforce the nearby Shortland Islands and Buin, in the south of Bougainville, taking troops from the west, where the US soldiers will soon land. Russian troops have forced the Germans out of the Crimea and most of the German troops on the left bank of the Dniepr by 30 October.

Bougainville is attacked on 1 November. As part of the 'island-hopping' plan, Bougainville gives access to the Japanese base at Rabaul, as well as airfields. There are 40,000 Japanese troops and 20,000 sailors on Bougainville, but they have mainly been pulled to the south of the island after the invasion of the Treasury Islands and the Americans land almost unopposed. The Japanese send a naval fleet to Bougainville to disrupt the landings. The three heavy cruisers, one light cruiser and six destroyers are attacked by US Navy ships. A light cruiser and destroyer are lost, while two heavy cruisers and a destroyer are damaged for the loss of

Above: Winston Churchill in charge of a 1943 strategy meeting with the figure of Jan Christian Smuts, the former Boer soldier who became a much-respected Field-Marshall when, as Prime Minister of South Africa, he threw in his lot with Great Britain again.

one damaged US ship. On the 5th, Rabaul is attacked by US ships, including two carriers, the *Saratoga* and *Princeton*. Ninety-seven aircraft attack the Japanese fleet at Rabaul. Eight cruisers and destroyers are damaged. The carriers *Bunker Hill*, *Essex* and *Independence* send off 183 aircraft to attack Rabaul on the 11th. They sink a light cruiser and a destroyer, with five other warships damaged. The Japanese have fifty-five aircraft destroyed in the attack too. Kiev is freed by the Russians on 6 November and the German 17th Army is now surrounded and holed up in the Crimea. There is no escape! Hitler has ordered that they shall not leave, but they can't anyway. The Soviets plan for the liberation of the western Ukraine as their next task. Kos is back under German control by 10 November. They plan to attack Leros and their landing craft are attacked by British destroyers. They still sail on 12 November for Leros and the Allies attempt to prevent the invasion. Air support and a landing by paratroops helps the German invasion. Arctic convoys resume on 15 November as the nights darken and the threat from the *Tirpitz* has dissipated. The war in Italy is slow and hard as the Allies have to fight for every inch of conquered ground.

Leros is captured on 16 November. The British have lost 4,800 men, twenty ships and 115 aircraft. The Germans have lost twelve merchant ships, twenty landing craft and have lost 4,000 troops. British aims to have a base in the Dodecanese have failed, primarily due to enemy air superiority and poor planning. Between 18 and 26 November, the Americans flush the Japanese out of Cibik Ridge, a heavily fortified and vital strategic position in Bougainville. Berlin is attacked on the night of 18 November, heralding the beginning of a five-month attack on the German capital. Thousands will die, and huge numbers will be made homeless. Between 20 and 23 November, the Americans land on the Gilbert Islands of Tarawa and Betio. 18,600 troops land after days of seaborne artillery bombardment. The 4,800 Japanese on the islands are buried deep underground in bunkers and few are killed in the bombardment. They appear and attack as the Americans land. The reefs surrounding the islands cause problems and the US troops have to wade ashore through the lagoons. The islands are captured by 23 November but 1,000 Americans die. Of the 4,800 Japanese, only 110 are captured.

The Allies are halted at the Gustav Line, as they advance towards Rome, but the British make a bridgehead over the Sangro River on 24 November. Roosevelt, Chiang Kai-shek and Churchill meet in Cairo on 22–26 November. A conference to discuss island-hopping in the Pacific is scheduled for 4–7 December. Makin island, occupied during the attacks on Tarawa and Betio, sees the loss of the US aircraft carrier *Liscombe Bay* on 24 November. A Japanese submarine sinks her with the loss of 644 sailors and airmen. The Japanese are less successful the following day, when they lose three ships during what will be the last sea battle of the Solomons campaign. The battle sees five US destroyers attack a Japanese surface fleet of destroyers and transports after the Japanese vessels have landed troops at Buka. Roosevelt, Churchill and Stalin all meet at Tehran, Iran, on 28 November. The Russians try and force a Second Front as soon as possible and details are agreed for Overlord and Anvil, the invasion of southern France.

December sees the creation of American airbases in Bougainville. Land bases make the success of the invasion guaranteed. On 20 December, the Huon Peninsula is pretty much under American control although Japanese resistance in pockets means mopping up operations need to take place in this part of Papua New Guinea throughout the rest of the month. On 24 December, General Dwight D. Eisenhower is announced as the commander of the forthcoming invasion of Europe. Air Chief Marshal Sir Arthur Tedder is Deputy Supreme Commander, while General Sir Henry Maitland becomes Supreme Allied Commander, Mediterranean. On Christmas Day, Allied forces land on New Britain and advance on Rabaul from the west. Boxing Day sees the German battleship *Scharnhorst* sunk in the Battle of the North Cape. The convoys JW-55B and RA-55A are defended by the British Home Fleet and the Germans are caught by surprise. The *Scharnhorst* is damaged, losing its fire control and radar first, then loses speed and finally meets her end by multiple torpedo strikes. Of her crew of 1,800, only thirty-six survive the freezing waters. The year ends with the basic planning for Operation Overlord agreed, the Germans surrounded in the Crimea, on the run in Italy and in Russia, the Italians now fighting with the Allies and the Japanese losing island after island in the Pacific. The war is by no means over but the tide has turned. Defeat for the Axis forces is guaranteed, the only question is when will they capitulate. On all fronts, the Allies are becoming accustomed to victory and the Axis forces to defeat.

JANUARY 1943

Above: A British Crusader tank on the Bou Arada road in Tunisia, which was the limit of the German tank patrol's sortie on 10 January. They were stopped by French and British troops mounting an attack from the outskirts of the town.

Above: The senior escort ship on a convoy, piled high with snow and ice, as seen through the ice-covered davits of a Canadian minesweeper.

Above: Encrusted in ice, a British destroyer during the bitterly cold winter of 1942/43. The destroyer rode out a gale of 60 to 70 mph while escorting a convoy to port. *Below:* A ship's lifeboat firmly encased in ice. Difficult enough to launch safely in ordinary conditions, it was now virtually unuseable. A silent tribute to the bravery of the sailors and seamen.

The arrival of supplies in Iceland. *Top:* A US Army Air Corps tanker being unloaded in typical Arctic weather. The ship had brought supplies for the US troops stationed on the island. *Bottom:* A Jeep driver is protected from the cold, with thick gloves, goggles and a sheepskin-lined coat.

Above: In the warmer climes of Casablanca, the seated figure of US President Roosevelt shakes hands with General Giraud, at that time Commander-in-Chief in French North Africa, together with General de Gaulle, the leader of the Fighting French with headquarters in London. British Prime Minister Winston Churchill looks on. The conference took place in French Morocco from 14–26 January 1943.

Pushing into Tunisia

Above: As the 8th Army advanced on Tripoli along the road between Beni Ulid and Tarhuna, this Bofors gun crew drive off a Stuka dive-bomber.

Left: A map of the Tunisia/Libya frontier showing the position of the Mareth Line. During January 1943 there was a stalemate in Tunisia which was not be resolved until Rommel's offensive in February.

Above: A line of Curtiss P-40 fighter-bomber aircraft in the desert. *Below:* A British vessel entering Tripoli harbour, the first to do so following the capitulation. In command was a Canadian officer, the second-in-command being a South African.

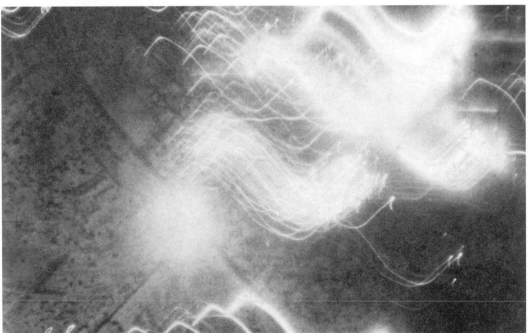

A daylight raid by Flying Fortresses on the Ateliers de Hallemes locomotive and wagon works in Lille, which took place on 13 January, is shown top. The lower photograph shows a night attack on the Daimler Benz factory in Berlin on the night of 17/18 January.

Opposite: Ruins of a school in Lewisham which was bombed on 21 January. Forty-two children and six teachers were killed. The British press made much of the Nazis attacking schools, but in reality there is no evidence to support such claims and the bombing was indiscriminate.

Above: An Allied bombing raid on the German submarine base at Lorient. The A, B and C indicate evidence of damage to a barracks and workshops, an officers' club which was gutted, an arsenal, the commander's offices, power station and repair shops which were also wrecked.

FEBRUARY 1943

The Kharkov area was a key point occupied by the Red Army on 16 February. The Russian infantry, shown here, are advancing between Kursk, which was captured on 8 February, and Kharkov.

The Eastern Front – Kharkov
Left: A map showing the front lines in the Kharkov area. It shows the Russian line at 16 February, with Kharkov within their territory. Kursk is shown to the north of Kharkov.

Below: A British cartoon by Illingworth, featuring the figure of Napoleon mocking Hitler for his failure to take Moscow.

By Illingworth

Above: During the liberation of Kharkov, Russian mortar squads are shown doubling through the streets during the final assault on the city on 16 February. *Below:* One of the city's squares piled up with debris from buildings destroyed by the retreating German forces.

Following on from the liberation of Leningrad, the Red Army consolidated its gains in the most northerly sector of the battlefront. In the harsh wintry conditions, machine-gunners are shown, above, while on patrol and, below, anti-tank guns and crews on the move in the central sector situated between Kursk and Kharkov.

Top: The corpse of a German soldier lies face down while a Russian tank moves forward. *Bottom:* A German tank, the only one saved from the work of saboteurs when they set fire to a granary which housed a number of tanks as well as a store of ammunition. In the background the pall of smoke from the burning building and equipment fills the sky.

Top left: A German soldier scans the horizon for signs of the Russians. *Top right:* This soldier, wounded in a battle near Lake Ilmen, is being led away from the front line for treatment. *Below:* A mounted soldier of the Waffen SS Cavalry Division exchanges greetings with a member of the Panzer Division in the struggle to stem the Russian advance in the Lake Ilmen area.

On the British Home Front
Top: Members of the OCTU are being given a practical lesson in minelaying during an exercise in the Southern Command. *Bottom:* The King inspects a division of the Royal Engineers who have demonstrated methods of purifying water, a sample of which he drank.

The War at Sea

Above: The paddle steamer *Lucy Ashton*, 16 February 1943. Many of Britain's pleasure steamers were redeployed during the war for a variety of roles including mine-sweeping duties.

Left: Flames and smoke issuing from a 7,000-ton Japanese supply ship attacked by US Army Air Force aircraft in the Bay of Bengal, off Rangoon, on 27 February. The crew can be seen taking to the boats.

Above: HMS *Onslow*, one of several destroyers which made contact with a heavy force of German warships off the North Cape, Norway, returns to port. She is clearly showing signs of the damage incurred and her funnel and bridge are riddled with splinter holes.

Battleships covered in ice. *Above:* The guns of a British battleship are caked with ice and snow after escorting a convoy from Britain to Russia by the northern route. *Below:* The seamen who served on these convoys experienced harsh conditions taking supplies through the Arctic Sea.

De-icing. Much of Canada's war production was aportioned between Britain and Russia. Shown above, a seaman is chipping ice from the ship's rail on a convoy about to set out from Canada to Russia.

The daylight air offensive continues. *Above:* Bombs from a Liberator aircraft of the USAAF bursting on the Trystian Lock on the approach channel at Dunkirk, and also on the quay west of the port. This raid took place on 13 February. *Below:* An RAF Ventura over Holland during an attack on the Royal Dutch Blast Furnaces and Steel Works at Ijmuiden, also on 13 February.

Above: A daylight attack on the U-boat base at St Nazaire. US bombers bombed the Atlantic submarine base on 16 February. *Below:* RAF bombers attacked Wilhelmshaven on 11 February. In this aerial photograph the devastation to the main depot at Meriensiel is plain to see. An area of around 150 acres was laid waste and storage tanks, shown bottom left, were damaged.

US fighter aircraft
Above: US Marine Air Force Wildcats at an airfield on Guadacanal. It is claimed that the US had shot down 876 Japanese aircraft by the end of February 1943.
Left and below: The mighty P-47 Thunderbolt. Airmen are shown examining three of the machine guns.

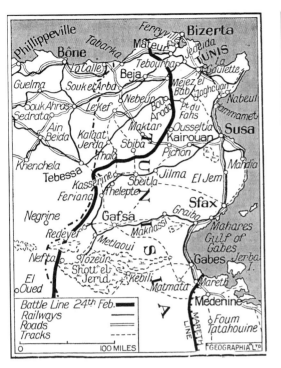

The Tunisian Campaign

Above left: A map of Tunisia showing the line to which the Allies had been pushed back by Rommel's Afrika Korps by 24 February. But the British cartoonists were in no doubt that events would go against the Germans in Tunisia, as this *Punch* cartoon by Bernard Partridge shows, above right. Under the headline 'Closing on Tunis', the Allied Armies have the German forces within their grasp. *Below:* Gordon Highlanders crossing the border from Tripolitania into Tunisia to bolster the forces for an assault on the Mareth Line. See also, page 24.

Top left: On a roadside in Tunisia, a sapper examines a clutch of abandoned German landmines and booby traps. These had not been laid in time before the 8th Army retook the area.

Middle left: The crew of a Sherman tank, which had taken part in an attack on a German position near Medjez-el-Bab, cleaning mud off the tracks and removing fouling from the gun.

Bottom left: Wrens, serving at the Allied Headquarters in North Africa, check their money very carefully as they purchase oranges from a street vendor.

Above: An abandoned German mobile gun found about 45 miles from Buerat. The trailer carried additional ammunition. *Below:* British artillerymen firing a 25-pounder on the road to Tripoli. Evidence of exploding shells can be seen in the background.

Malta
A march-past of British infantry on the island as they set off on a large-scale practice attack. Note the elaborately camouflaged staff car for Brigidier Kenneth Pierce Smith, who is taking the salute.

MARCH 1943

Above: An Avro Lancaster bomber forms the centrepiece of the opening ceremony of the Wings for Victory Week, on 6 March 1943. The event was marked by the release of 1,300 pigeons carrying messages to all parts of the country.

The War in the East
Left: The battle-line on the Russian front from Lake Ilmen to Rostov, at 23 March 1943.

Below: Russian marines serving with a commando unit on the Black Sea after a raid on an Axis-held port. Motor launches have laid a smoke-screen, seen in the background, to protect the ships.

Above: Men of the Red Army attacking during the final stages of the Russian winter offensive. It is estimated that nearly a million troops of both sides were killed in the southern campaign in Russia. More than a quarter of a million others were taken prisoner. *Below:* A typical Cossack family – Alexander, a machine-gunner, Ninel, a medical instructor, Natalia, another machine-gunner, their mother Yevdokia, army cook, and their father Gordei Zubenko, who was an instructor with a guards unit.

Action in Tunisia
Top: Infantry of the 1st Army making their way through a cornfield north of Bou Arada.
Bottom: A 105-mm Howitzer Motor Carriage M7 – widely known as a 'Priest' because of its circular gun ring – mounted on an M3 medium tank chassis. It is shown being camouflaged before an attack near Bou Arada.

Above: An 8th Army Bren Carrier leaving Ben Ulid on a coastal road in the southern area of the Tunis campaign. *Below:* A 90-mm anti-aircraft abandoned by the Italians during the retreat from Tripoli.

Above: Sappers shown removing mines from the Castel Benito airfield in Tripoli. One man is using a mine-detector while his companion removes the mines by hand. *Below:* A hill-top observation post with a British soldier watching German troop movements near the town of Mateur, a key town in the north of the Tunisian tip.

Allied Air Power

Above: Men of the Royal Canadian Air Force, which had formerly been under RAF command before operating within the RCAF Bomber Group.

Right: Crew of a Halifax of the Ceylon Squadron studying a map before embarking on an operational flight. These men had been on raids to Berlin, Essen, Kiel and other targets within Germany.

Above: A twin-engined Airspeed Oxford, used in the training of bomber pilots. The aircrew received initial training at special RAF training fields before moving on to operational training units. *Below:* New armaments for the Flying Fortress. A gunner in the nose is shown firing one of the two additional machine guns.

Top: The pilot of an RAF Army Co-operation Command Mustang being briefed for an operation. The Air Liaison Officer of the ACC is a soldier. *Bottom:* Loading the 20-mm Hispano cannon of an RAF Whirlwind fighter-bomber. The Whirlwinds were active in attacking locomotives, goods trains, power stations and communications infrastructure in occupied countries, and enemy shipping in coastal waters.

On the Burma Front
Above: Members of the Royal Indian Army Service Corps wading through a river with their mules. They are following the river bed rather than hack their way through the jungle.

Gradually new roads were created through the difficult and often mountainous jungle terrain in Burma. Chinese labourers and mules made the preliminary tracks, above, followed by the bulldozers and road-making machinery. This is the Ledo road, which was completed as far as the Hukawng Valley by the end of 1943.

Below: A map of the battle area in Burma, 1943.

The Far East
Top left: Natives of the Sanananda area of Papua New Guinea carrying a wounded soldier on a stretcher through the jungle. *Top right:* A captured naval gun in a Japanese emplacement at Buna, New Guinea. *Bottom:* US Marines who have fought in Guadalcanal are shown passing along a new road carved through the jungle.

Home Front

Above: 'May Day in Merrie England, 1943.' A cartoon reflecting the changing face of country life. *Below:* General Sir Bernard Paget inspects airborne troops. The aircraft is a Horsa glider. 1943 saw an extensive period of preparation and training for the landings to come in 1944.

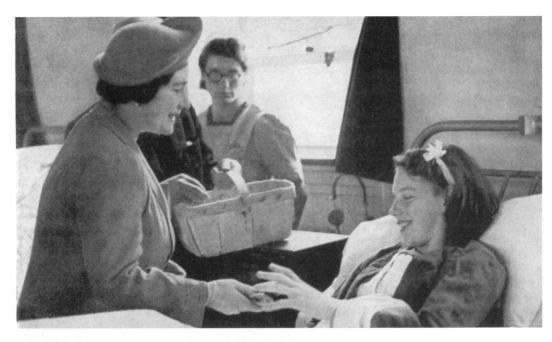

Women in the War

Above: In a hospital ward in Lewisham, the Queen presents Edith Wilson, a casualty of an air raid on London, with one of the bananas brought back from Casablanca by Lord Louis Mountbatten as a present for the Princesses Elizabeth and Margaret.

Left: Members of the ATS 'manning' a sound locator. The women played an important role in Britain's anti-aircraft defences.

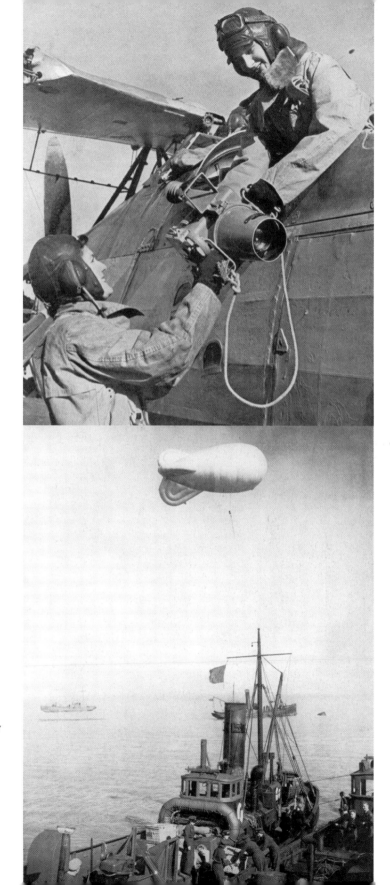

Right: A Fleet Air Arm Wren taking a camera onboard an aircraft in a photographic training exercise.

Bottom right: Members of the Women's Auxiliary Air Force loading a tug with supplies for the barrage balloon-carrying barges. WAAFs had been working in Balloon Command since 1941.

Top: A girl cutting plates in a British shipyard in the North-East, using an oxy-acetylene burner. 'Her work is typical of the many jobs connected with the war effort that the woman of Britain are engaged on.' *Bottom:* Women also worked in the factories of Canada. This woman is operating equipment for the production of cartridges.

APRIL 1943

Germany's revolutionary jet-powered fighter/bomber, the Messerschmitt Me 262, went into full-scale production at the end of 1943. Shown above is V2, the 'V' standing for *Versuchsmuster* or 'experimental/test' aircraft, which crashed on 18 April 1943. Note the rear tail-dragger landing gear configuration with the nose pointing upwards. This was later changed to the more familiar tricycle undercarriage with a nose wheel, and by the time that the Me 262 V3 was demonstrated to Adolf Hitler at the Interburg airfield on 26 November this was fully retractable. Although won over by the Me 262's obvious advantages in terms of speed and performance, Hitler stipulated that it should be deployed as a *Schnellbomber*, a 'Fast Bomber', rather than as a defensive fighter.

Allied Advance in Tunisia
Above: The body of a German soldier lies where he had fallen on a Mark III tank knocked out in the Allied advance on Thala. *Below:* Italian troops surrender to the men of the 8th Army.

A patriotic portrait of Franklin Delano Roosevelt. It was President Roosevelt who, following the Japanese air attack on the American fleet at Pearl Harbor in December 1941, brought the USA into the Second World War as a combatant on the Allied side.

Seawomen of BOAC

British Overseas Airway Corporation employed a number of 'seawomen' to work the launches used to service the four-engined Boeing 314 Clipper flying-boats coming in from West Africa, Lisbon and the USA. The launches required skilful handling, especially in bad weather, to come alongside the easily-damaged aircraft. The women, whose ages ranged from twenty-three to thirty-eight, were promoted to coxwain and placed in charge of a launch after they had successfully completed three months' training in Morse code, semaphore and lamp signalling, compass work and general seamanship. Their duties included embarking and disembarking passengers and handling the launch while stevedores loaded and unloaded mail and freight.

These photographs, left, show BOAC coxwains leaving the flying-boat *Berwick*, and also signalling to the shore from the nose of the aircraft.

Above: The big Heinkel He 115 has been described as the Luftwaffe's most successful attack and reconnaissance seaplane. Around 500 were built. *Below:* The Arado Ar 196 reconnaissance floatplane. A conventional low-wing monoplane, the Ar 196 became the standard aircraft of the Kriegsmarine throughout the war. It was launched from a ship via a catapult system.

Action in Sicily
Quieter scenes from the campaign in Sicily. British troops of the 78th Infantry Division are shown left, about to sample an evening brew made over a camp fire.

Below: Two wounded soldiers smile cheerfully for the camera as they await evacuation from an advanced dressing post. Nearly all Sicilian battle casualties were evacuated by air, and by 14 August 1943 almost 15,000 sick and wounded men had been flown to hospitals in North Africa.

Mussolini Escapes

Top: In 1943 the Germans' Operation Eiche saw a Fieseler Storch Fi 156 used to rescue the deposed Italian dictator Benito Mussolini from a mountaintop near the Gran Sasso. Although the mountain was surrounded by Italian forces, German paratroops and commandos under the command of Otto Skorzeny captured the site, which had only a limited landing space for the light aircraft. Despite being overloaded, with Mussolini and Skorzeny aboard, the Fieseler took off in just 250 feet.

Right: General Bernard Law Montgomery, commander of the 8th Army from August 1942 to December 1943, when he was appointed Commander-in-Chief of the British Group of Armies being organised in the UK for the forthcoming liberation of Europe.

War in the Air – the Allied Aircraft
Top: The all-metal Boeing Fortress II, popularly known as the Flying Fortress. It had a crew of nine and was powered by four Wright Double Row Cyclone engines. *Bottom:* The Hawker Typhoon was one of Britain's most heavily armed and armoured fighter aicraft.

Above: Britain's De Havilland Mosquito, a two-seat reconnaissance bomber of all-wooden construction. Powered by two Rolls-Royce liquid-cooled engines, it was fast with a speed of almost 400 mph and, consequently, could penetrate enemy territory without a fighter escort.

Below: The distinctive twin-fuselage configuration of the Lockheed Lighting, which had come into RAF service in 1942 and was highly effective in the Tunisian campaign.

German Anti-Aircraft Defences

The Flakartillerie units of the Luftwaffe had an increasingly vital role to play in defending the Reich from enemy bombers. The propaganda photographs published at the time, shown above, were intended to reassure the civilian population that their safety was in good hands. The crew of an 88-mm flak gun battery are shown responding to a siren signifying approaching aircraft. Throughout the war the Germans had almost twice as many anti-aircraft guns as Britain. The Flakartillerie was under the control of the Luftwaffe, which coordinated defences, and by August 1944 there were almost 11,000 guns in service.

The War at Sea

Above: The sinking of the *Scharnhorst*, 26 December 1943. The battleship had long been a threat to British shipping and her loss left the German navy with six heavy units. Completed in 1939, *Scharnhorst* had a speed of 27 knots and carried nine 11-inch guns, twelve 5.9-inch guns and thirty others.

Middle right: RAF Air-Sea rescue launches portrayed in Stephen Bone's painting *The Fish Quay Beyond.*

Bottom right: A British corvette on convoy protection has shot down a Heinkel He 111 torpedo aircraft. The well-armed corvettes were portrayed as 'U-boat killers' that could also defend against aerial raiders. 'The pilot's dinghy has become swamped, and a rescue boat is being lowered.' Note the depth charges lined up in the stern chute.

The Art of War
Throughout the war years British artists portrayed many aspects of the action, both in the field and on the Home Front. *Above: Dressing Station*, by Reginald Mills. *Below:* Basutos deal with overflow mail on the causeway, Valetta, painted by Leslie Cole.

Above: Henry Carr's dramatic image of a *Parachute Drop*. *Below:* Workers at the Woolwich Arsenal in 1943, in a painting by Robert Austin.

Luftwaffe Maritime Patrols

The four-engine Focke-Wulf Fw 200, known as the 'Condor', was originally developed as an airliner. In its military form it served as a long-range reconnaissance and anti-shipping patrol and attack aircraft, and also as a transport. *Below:* A crew prepares for an Atlantic patrol.

On the Eastern Front

Above: Aircrew walking to a line of Fw 200 Condors which stand in readiness. The Fw 200 was used to transport supplies into Stalingrad, and in the later stages of the war the aircraft came to be used solely for transportation, its role as a reconnaissance aircraft taken over by the Junkers Ju 290. *Below:* Loading a Heinkel He 111 with a 250-kg bomb.

Appeals by Poster
These posters reflect the varying messages aimed at the British public on the Home Front during 1943–44. As the nature of the threat changed the emphasis was less on the propaganda messages of the earlier war years and instead they are in the form of appeals and information. Instructions include 'Cover Your Hair for Safety', 'Talk Less', 'Look Out for Children', 'Don't Touch', and 'Salute the Soldier'.

A further selection on similar themes. 'Your Talk May Kill Your Comrades', Guard Your Tongue' and 'Tickets into Bullets – Used Tickets are Munitions of War – Put Yours in the Box'.

BOMB DISPOSAL-ARMY

ARMY
CATERING
CORPS

ROYAL ARTILLERY
(Sergeants, Battery
Quartermaster
Sergeants &
Sergeants, A.T.S.)

KINGS BADGE
for Invalided

ARMY DRIVERS
(Proficiency)

EAGLE SQUADRON-R.A.F.

PIONEER CORPS

AIR
GUNNER

PARACHUTE TROOPS

RECONNAISSANCE
CORPS

COMMANDO
TROOPS

ROYAL NAVAL
PATROL SERVICE — Gunnery
Instructor

BOMB DISPOSAL-
R.A.F.

MINESWEEPERS
Petty Officer

Wartime Badges of Britain's Armed Forces

All of the badges shown here were introduced between September 1939 and December 1941 and remained in use throughout the remainder of the war. All were worn on the sleeve except for those of the Army Catering Corps, Pioneer Corps, Reconnaissance Corps (worn on cap), Air Gunner (on left breast), and the King's Badge for men and women invalided from the armed forces (in coat lapel). The Eagle Squadron, which operated within the RAF, was composed exclusively of American fighter pilots.

Above left: German prisoners taken in the attack on Pichon being allowed to retrieve their water bottles. *Top right:* Captured at Kairouan, these prisoners are taken to a camp. *Below:* British troops inspect a German 75-mm anti-tank gun mounted on a self-propelling chassis.

Above: British units of the 8th Army head northwards after occupying Kairouan on 11 April. The town is midway between Pichon and Susa. *Below:* On the outskirts of Kairouan, an 8th Army gunner directs convoys past German vehicles wrecked in the battle for the town.

General Alexander, deputy Commander-in-Chief North Africa, is shown above addressing British and American war correspondents at an open-air conference held at his headquarters in northern Tunisia. *Below:* Seized on by the propagandists, another photograph of a dead German and a knocked-out tank. He died in an attack north-west of Medinine.

The hero of the
Tunisia campaign,
General Montgomery,
acknowledges the
greetings of the crowd
at Susa. In the back of
the Jeep are bouquets
presented to him.
The cartoon, inset,
is by Gittins and is
captioned 'Monty pulls
the strings'.

Spitfires in the desert. *Top:* The pilots enjoy an interval of quiet on a forward airfield in Tunisia. They are dressed in their flying gear, ready for action at any moment. *Bottom:* A Spitfire ready to take off from a runway made of coir matting covered with a Somerfeld track which consists of metal rods about 9 inches apart and spaced with wire netting.

Top: The hospital ship *Atlantis* arriving at a British port with men who were wounded during the Libyan campaign. These were the more serious cases who had been treated at base hospitals until well enough for the voyage home. *Bottom:* Some of the wounded settled in a hospital train. *Opposite page:* There is no doubting the relief felt by these men as the *Atlantis* docks back in England.

Above: RAF Boston bombers on an operational flight over Tunisia, where almost continuous attacks were made against Axis-held airfields. The raids intensified as the Allied troops moved nearer to Tunis itself. *Below:* Aircraft of the north-west African air forces were also attacking airfields in Sicily. This is the airfield in Milo, hit on 5 April. Around thirty aircraft, many of them Junkers Ju 52 transports, were destroyed on the ground and many others damaged.

MAY 1943

The captain, and first mate, of a Soviet ship plying the Amur River, which borders Manchuria and feeds into the Sea of Okhotsk. As Josef Stalin stated in the conclusion to his May Day address, 'Hitlerite Germany and her armies are shaken and are undergoing a crisis, but they are not yet defeated. It would be naïve to suppose that the catastrophe will come of its own accord as part of the normal course of events. Two or three more such powerful blows are necessary from west and east as have been inflicted on the Hitlerite armies during the past five or six months, so that the catastrophe facing Hitlerite Germany may become a fact. Therefore, the people of our Soviet Union and the Red Army, as well as our armies, still have to face a hard and severe struggle. This struggle will demand from them great sacrifices, enormous staying power and iron stamina. They will have to mobilise all their power to smash the enemy and thus pave the way to peace.'

Tunis Falls on 7 May 1943
Above: This aerial photograph, taken shortly after the occupation, shows that Tunis had survived relatively unscathed by Allied bombing. *Below:* A broad smile on the face of this British soldier tells it all as he enters Tunis to the hearty acclaim of the inhabitants.

Evidence of the hard fighting in the Tunis area. *Top left:* The bodies of two German soldiers killed in battle near El Aroussa lying by the Medjez-el-Bab roadside. *Top right:* An ammunition container dropped by parachute to the Axis forces. *Below:* A large German half-track captured by the British in the North African desert. These were used to transport guns and personnel.

Above: French citizens wave the Tricolor as the Allies enter Tunis, May 1943. *Below:* A German gunner's grave in the desert, beside the 88-mm artillery gun and a wrecked tank.

Above: A British newsreel photo of General Alexander, Deputy Commander-in-Chief North Africa, driving a Jeep only a few miles from the front line during a visit to the advanced brigade headquarters in Tunisia. *Below:* Another German 88-mm gun, this time about to be towed away from the battlefield near El Aroussa.

Above: A vast number of prisoners, Italian and German, captured in or around Tunis. During the last stages in the thrust for the city the prisoners were coming in at a rate of 1,000 an hour. *Below:* A British soldier drives a captured German car loaded with prisoners.

Above: Watched by two members of the Allied armies, American and British ships anchor in Bizerta harbour. *Below*: Truckloads of Italians captured during the Tunisia campaign on their way to Tunis from a temporary camp. They appear to be pleased that the fighting is over.

Among the vast array of equipment abandoned by the Germans was this Junkers Ju 90 transport aircraft, shown above. It was not uncommon for captured equipment, including aircraft, to be reused by the other side. *Below:* Cape Bon, described in the original caption for this photograph as the 'Land's End' of Tunisia. Across the Mediterranean is Italy, a stepping-stone to victory.

More wrecks, this time of fighter aircraft.

Main picture: A French soldier examines a German Messerschmitt Bf 109 fighter at what appears to be an aircraft graveyard on the airfield at El Aoulana. There is the fuselage of a Junkers Ju 52 in the background.

Inset, right: The remains of the tail section of a French aircraft found on a captured airfield.

Above: Having safely arrived at a North African port this oil tanker brings fresh fuel supplies for the Allies. *Below:* One of the many dumps of arms and ammunition abandoned by the Germans in Tunisia. There are a variety of guns and, in the background, a number of vehicles.

Above: The band of the Anti-Tank Regiment playing at a thanksgiving service held in the ancient ruins of the amphitheatre at Carthage. It was attended by the officers and men of the 1st Army, shown below, and General Anderson read the lesson.

The Dambusters Raid

In the early morning of 17 May, a force of nineteen Lancaster bombers led by Wing-Commander Gibson delivered a devastaing blow on the Ruhr Dams. Using Barnes Wallis's bouncing bombs they breached the Moehne Dam, top left, as well as the Eder Dam, resulting in flooding in the Ruhr Valley, shown at the bottom. They also damaged the railway viaduct near Herdecke, top right. Other dams were attacked in a second wave but not breached below the water line. Eight Lancs were lost, fifty-three crew died.

The ground staff were the unsung heroes of the bombing campaign. *Above:* While the flight crew looks on, the engineers attend to the engines on this Avro Lancaster bomber. *Below:* Gunners of a B-17 Flying Fortress perch on ammunition boxes containing 46,000 rounds of .5 cannon shells, sufficient to arm seven aircraft. At the front a bombadier sits astride a 2,000-lb bomb.

Above: A mobile blacksmith's workshop, where repairs could be carried out in the field by craftsmen of the Royal Electrical & Mechanical Engineers (REME). This example was photographed in Tunisia, and there were other types equipped with lathes or for tinsmiths, welders and wireless mechanics.

JUNE 1943

Above: Mishaps were not uncommon on the US aircraft carriers. Here a Douglas Dauntless has ended up with its tail pointed in the air and its nose on the carrier deck. The photograph was taken in the Pacific on 21 June 1943.

An RAF Ventura bomber shown over its target, the shipyards at Flushing, on 24 June, when a formation of these aircraft made an attack on the De Schelde shipbuilding yards. Smoke can be seen rising from the engine shops of the marine docks and also from oil storage tanks.

Right: Wing-Commander C. D. Tomalin, a well known pre-war diving champion, climbs aboard his Mosquito prior to a night intruder mission. This type of aircraft had brought Berlin within reasonable striking range.

Below: A Halifax bomber, which has sustained damage from enemy flak during a raid over Germany, is receiving attention. The mechanics will soon have the aircraft ready to return to its duties.

Taking the Sicilian Islands

Above left: Admiral Pavesi, Italian Commander-in-Chief of Pantellaria, together with another captured officer. The island had fallen on 11 June following a round-the-clock bombardment. *Above right*: The commander of the Lampedusa garrison, who surrendered the island after only a brief resistance. *Below*: Damage caused by the Allied bombardment of the airfield at Lampedusa.

Above: Allied engineers immediately went to work at Pantellaria. No time was wasted in clearing away the debris at the dock area.

Above: Another view of the damage caused at the Pantellaria airfield. These wrecks are Italian aircraft. *Below:* British troops on Pantellaria passing by a blazing petrol dump. At the front is Lance-Sergeant A. Haywood, a Sheffield man, who was awarded the Military Medal for his part in an action in Tunisia.

JULY 1943

The landings on Sicily on 10 July 1943 marked the Allies' long-awaited return to Europe. *Above:* While an M7 Priest wades ashore British soldiers form a human chain to land ammunition brought on the landing craft.

Sicily – The Vanguard

On 10 July 1943, British, Canadian and US troops, with naval and air support, took part in the greatest combined operation of the war so far. *Above:* These British soldiers are seen boarding their landing craft. *Below:* A map of the Italian island of Sicily, which is roughly the size of Wales. It was regarded by the Allies as a stepping stone to the mainland of Fortress Europe.

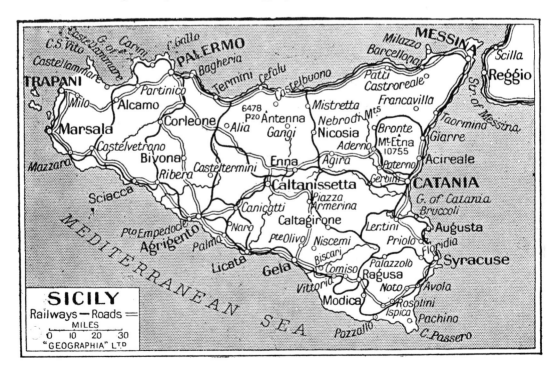

Top: Landing craft laden with troops ready for the assault, with several others in the background already on their way. The Allied landing, on a 100-mile front, began before dawn. *Bottom:* Crowded with troops, this landing craft is about to land on the Sicilian beaches.

Above: These Canadiain soldiers are listening to a briefing while on board ship on their way to Sicily. *Below:* Only a few hours into the invasion and supplies are being brought ashore, passed from landing craft to beach by a human chain. Meanwhile other men smooth out the beach.

Above: 8th Army troops and a Sherman tank are passing through Pachino, which was cleared of the enemy on 12 July, just two days after the landings. Its capture was one of the early successes of the Sicilian campaign. *Below:* Soldiers march through Noto on the way to Syracuse. The seaport is connected by the railway running from Pachino.

The Sicilian landings were an opportunity for the Allies to put their landing techniques to the test. *Above:* A landing craft disgorges two British tanks directly on to the beach. *Below:* General Montgomery rides in one of the DUKW amphibious landing craft used in the landings.

The DUKW amphibious landing craft became one of the most recognisable vehicles of the D-Day landings on the beaches of Normandy in June 1944, as shown above.

Preparing to fight on the Beaches

Wars have seen great technological advances in short periods of time as money, resources and skilled labour are put to the task of developing weapons of war. 1943 saw numerous new weapons come to the battlefield. Some, like the Panjandrum, a rocket-propelled axle, powered like a Catherine Wheel and filled with deadly high explosives, were deemed so unsafe, they were never used in battle. Others, like the DUKW, have entered popular folklore and are still a regular sight at military shows the world over, with 21,147 produced and a hundred or more still in existence and even in military service.

The DUKW itself came about as a result of the need to attack enemy-held coastlines in Europe via the beaches rather than the ports, which were expected to be heavily defended and to suffer untold damage at the hands of their defenders and in the assaults needed to capture them. It was designed by Rod Stephens Jr, who was employed by Sparkman & Stephens, yacht designers, Dennis Puleston and Frank W. Speir, from MIT. Initially ignored by the US services, it was the rescue of seven stranded US Coast Guardsmen from their beached craft, stuck on a sandbank in 60-knot winds, by a passing experimental DUKW that saw the DUKW be accepted as a potential solution to the problem of supplying troops on beaches.

The DUKW was loosely based around the mechanicals of a General Motors Corporation 6x6 truck, the GMS AFKWX, a cab-over-engine version of the ubiquitous 'Big Jimmy'. Around the mechanicals was built a watertight hull, with revised machinery, that included a propeller drive to the rear. To go into production, the final design tweaks were made by the Yellow Truck & Coach Co., of Pontiac, Michigan. Weighing in at 6.5 tons empty, the truck, powered by a 4,425 cc petrol engine, was capable of a top speed of 50 mph on the road and around 5.5 knots in the water. The DUKW was not a small vehicle, being 31 feet long, almost 8 feet 3 inches wide and nearly 9 feet high. It was not armoured, despite its looks, and had a high-capacity bilge pump fitted to ensure it would stay afloat if hit by small-calibre weapons. Over 5,000 were fitted with a 0.5-inch Browning machine gun. The DUKW had a unique feature in that its tyres could be inflated or deflated by the driver to suit the terrain.

The first DUKWs were sent to the Pacific theatre, in particular Guadalcanal, but were first used in anger at the invasion of Sicily in the summer of 1943. They proved invaluable in the attack on Sicily and helped supply the beachheads with ammunition and other supplies, as well as recover the injured back to ships offshore. Britain acquired 2,000 DUKWs under Lend-Lease, while 535 were sold to Australian forces for use in the Pacific. Russia received 586 and built a reverse-engineered version after the war.

In wartime service, DUKWs were used in the Mediterranean, during the D-Day landings, with some crossing the Channel under their own power, and during late 1944 and 1945 during the Battle of the Scheldt, Operation Veritable and Operation Plunder.

The DUKW brought to life the concept of an amphibious vehicle that could be used on land and also at sea, and helped make the invasions of Southern Europe and Normandy possible. Without its flexibility, the invasions could not have been so successful so quickly. However, the DUKW was just one of many successful weapons created in 1943, another being the Sherman DD or Duplex Drive tank, which could also float. With a flotation screen, they were developed by April 1943, and saw action during D-Day and subsequently during the invasion of Southern France and in Operation Plunder, the British crossing of the Rhine in 1945.

Equipment for arrival by air was also under development. *Above left:* A British airborne soldier carrying a portable wireless set. *Above right:* A new type of folding bicycle, also part of the equipment issued to the airborne soldiers. *Below:* A paratroop holding his 'wellbike', a motor scooter small enough to fit folded up inside a container and dropped by parachute.

Above: The RAF bombed the city of Hamburg over four nights, creating a firestorm that killed an estimated 50,000. *Below and right:* Berlin blazing later in 1943 after a bombing raid with British phosphorous bombs.

A German poster for the benefit of the civilian population, *Der Fiend sieht Dein Licht! Verdunkeln!* 'The Enemy Sees Your Lights! Blackout!'

When the Allied bombers attacked Cologne on 3 July they also visited Kalk and Deutz, two industrial districts on the east bank of the Rhine. *Above:* The Klockner Humboldt-Deutz works, which produced diesel engines for the U-boats. *Below:* The district of Kalk took a heavy battering with the marshalling yards and the Kalk chemical factory taking hits.

AUGUST 1943

Above: Progressing cautiously over rising ground and taking advantage of what little cover is provided by the stubble, this Red Army trench-mortar crew is moving forward to engage the enemy.

The Russian Offensive

Above: These Russian infantrymen are breaking through barbed-wire defences in their advance against the retreating German forces. For the first time in the war the Red Army had staged a summer offensive. *Below:* Red Army scouts use a periscope and binoculars to make a survey of the German lines in the Orel area.

Raid on Ploesti
On the afternoon of 1 August 1943, 200 American Liberators made a spectacular low-level raid on the Rumanian oil refineries at Ploesti. The refineries were the source of nearly half of Germany's oil supplies. *Top left:* A Liberator over the refineries. *Top right:* A fire at the Creditul Minier plant. *Bottom:* Three of the Liberators flying between the columns of dark smoke.

Advances in Sicily
Above: A British gun crew drives through the streets of Catania, which fell into Allied hands four days after the offensive launched on 1 August. *Below:* Sherman tanks pass through the Via Garibaldi in the centre of the town.

Above: Men of the 8th Army marching through the same street in Catania. This is the first British patrol since the town fell on 5 August. *Below:* The patrol continues into a more badly damaged area near the centre of the town. At least the wall of this bombed building, with its shattered statues, provides some welcome cover for the patrol.

There had been considerable resistance before Catania was taken and these British soldiers, above, are undertaking a close search for enemy troops in hiding. *Below:* After the departure of the Axis forces, and before the Allies could establish law and order, the looters ran riot for a time. Here they are ransacking shops, throwing food and clothes into the streets.

Top right: A sight that would become familiar in the towns of Sicily following the Allied invasion. Police and civilians of Noto, one of the earliest of the towns captured, take interest in the first proclamation issued by General Alexander.

Lower right: Taking up their quarters in a battle-scarred farmhouse near Cosmiso airfield, this mobile RAF operations unit gets down to work.

Below: A US Flying Fortress attacks Messina. The fall of Messina on 17 August signalled the fall of Sicily itself.

Operation Crossbow - The Raid on Peenemünde

Hitler had intended that his Vengeance weapons, the V1 flying-bomb and the V2 ballistic rocket, would reign terror down upon London and turn the course of the war in Germany's favour. In fact it wouldn't be until June 1944 that the first V1 – or 'Doodlebug' as they became known – fell on the capital, and the V2 followed three months after that, by which time it was too late to make a difference to the inevitable outcome of the war. The Allies knew that Germany was developing new weapons, and it was through the painstaking examination of aerial reconnaissance photographs that Peenemünde, located on Germany's Baltic coast, was identified as the major centre for research and development of rockets. On the night of 17/18 August 1943, almost 600 RAF bombers attacked Peenemünde, dropping 1,593 tons of high explosives, killing around 732 of Peenemünde's staff, some of them foreign workers. The RAF lost forty bombers in the raid. Throughout the remainder of the year further Operation Crossbow raids were carried out against the V-weapon launch sites which were under construction in northern France. While it is extimated that the Peenemünde raid only delayed development of the V-weapons by a number of weeks, it did force the Germans to move their factories underground and, in the case of the V2, to develop mobile launch systems.

Below: One of the aerial reconnaissance photographs that revealed the presence of the test launch area and also a number of rockets at the top-secret Peenemünde site on the edge of the Baltic. Although Londoners would not become familiar with either of the Vengeance weapons, the V1 or V2, until 1944, such intelligence enabled the RAF to disrupt their development.

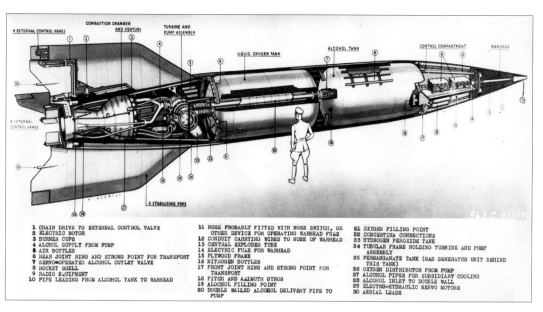

4 EXTERNAL CONTROL VANES · COMBUSTION CHAMBER AND VENTURI · TURBINE AND PUMP ASSEMBLY · LIQUID OXYGEN TANK · ALCOHOL TANK · CONTROL COMPARTMENT · WARHEAD · 4 INTERNAL CONTROL VANES · 4 STABILISING FINS

1 CHAIN DRIVE TO EXTERNAL CONTROL VALVE
2 ELECTRIC MOTOR
3 BURNER CUPS
4 ALCOHOL SUPPLY FROM PUMP
5 AIR BOTTLES
6 REAR JOINT RING AND STRONG POINT FOR TRANSPORT
7 SERVO-OPERATED ALCOHOL OUTLET VALVE
8 ROCKET SHELL
9 RADIO EQUIPMENT
10 PIPE LEADING FROM ALCOHOL TANK TO WARHEAD

11 NOSE PROBABLY FITTED WITH NOSE SWITCH, OR OTHER DEVICE FOR OPERATING WARHEAD FUZE
12 CONDUIT CARRYING WIRES TO NOSE OF WARHEAD
13 CENTRAL EXPLODER TUBE
14 ELECTRIC FUZE FOR WARHEAD
15 PLYWOOD FRAME
16 NITROGEN BOTTLES
17 FRONT JOINT RING AND STRONG POINT FOR TRANSPORT
18 PITCH AND AZIMUTH GYROS
19 ALCOHOL FILLING POINT
20 DOUBLE WALLED ALCOHOL DELIVERY PIPE TO PUMP

21 OXYGEN FILLING POINT
22 CONCERTINA CONNECTIONS
23 HYDROGEN PEROXIDE TANK
24 TUBULAR FRAME HOLDING TURBINE AND PUMP ASSEMBLY
25 PERMANGANATE TANK (GAS GENERATOR UNIT BEHIND THIS TANK)
26 OXYGEN DISTRIBUTOR FROM PUMP
27 ALCOHOL PIPES FOR SUBSIDIARY COOLING
28 ALCOHOL INLET TO DOUBLE WALL
29 ELECTRO-HYDRAULIC SERVO MOTORS
30 AERIAL LEADS

An Allied intelligence drawing of the V2 rocket, above, and a rocket being prepared for launch, shown on the right.

Below: Cutaway of the Luftwaffe's Vengeance weapon, the pilotless glide-bomb designated as the V1. These were mostly launched via ramps, located in northern France, pointed towards their target, usually London.

Landings in the Pacific
Above: Canadian and US troops boarding a landing craft which took part in the Kiska Island landing on 15 August – a bloodless victory as the Japanese had fled. *Below:* Machine gunners in action during the march on Mubo, in New Guinea, following the landing at Nassau Bay.

SEPTEMBER 1943

Above: American soldiers proceed with caution across a square in Acerno, Italy, occupied on 22 September. Apart from the abandoned equipment, in this case an 88-mm gun, there was no sign of the enemy.

The Invasion of Italy

On 3 September the Allies landed on the 'toe' of Italy. *Above:* A newswire photograph of landing craft on the beach near Reggio. This was among the first towns to be occupied. *Below:* British troops come ashore at Gallico Marina, a few miles to the north of Reggio.

Above left: The people of Reggio extend a warm welcome to this Sherman tank crew as they enter the town. *Above right:* A map of the invasion zones showing the three lines of advance by 14 September. *Below:* An M7 Priest self-propelled 105-mm Howitzer Motor Carriage disembarking from a landing craft during the operations in southern Italy.

Above: With Macchi fighters as the background, Italian and British airmen line up to be photographed at Brindisi airfield, which was captured on 11 September. *Below:* The muscular lines of a Luftwaffe Focke-Wulf Fw 190 left intact at the aerodrome at Montecorvino, complete with its bomb load in place. Other bombs lie in the foreground.

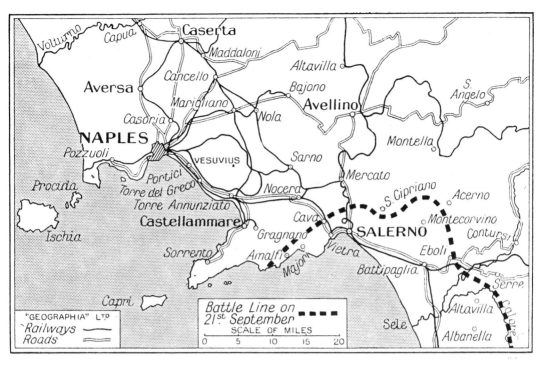

Above: A more detailed map of the area of operation at Salerno, showing the battle line on 21 September. *Below:* Having secured their positions the men of the 5th Army fought into the hills. They are shown stacking ammunition for their 105-mm guns as they make ready for action.

Above: With tank obstacles to either side, British infantry of the 5th Army pass through a street in Salerno. *Below:* A Bren carrier negotiating the debris-strewn streets in Salerno.

Another town, another day. Troops of the 8th Army are leaving Rosarno, above. Their advance was delayed by the enemy's demolition of road bridges in the area. *Below:* When Taranto fell into British hands it was found that the airfield was littered with the wrecks of German aircraft. Here an RAF officer examines the remains of a Junkers Ju 52 three-engined transport.

Above: Watched by the inhabitants of Resina, Allied vehicles squeeze past the heaps of rubble. Resina was the last town to be occupied before Naples. *Below:* Wreckage in the harbour at Messina, with the funnel of a merchant vessel bombed by the Allies showing above the water.

Pacific Operations

Above: Stretcher cases among the US forces which invaded New Georgia being loaded on to a barge for transport to a hospital. *Below:* Gunners in action in New Guinea, firing at the Japanese positions on Mount Tambu. The gun, its separate parts weighing up to 250 lbs, had to be man-handled across the steep and difficult jungle terrain.

Left: US Marines in the Pacific theatre indulge in a bathe in a stream while an alert machine-gunner keeps watch for any sign of the enemy.

Below: Supplies being brought ashore on an island in the south-west Pacific. The amphibious vehicle is an amphibious Buffalo, a type of small landing craft.

British Warships
Above: A Royal Navy battleship of the HMS *King George V* Class, accompanied by a destroyer, maintains a sunset vigil in 'northern waters'. *Below:* Hoisting a depth-charge into the ready position on board the corvette HMS *Widgeon*, on convoy escort duty in the North Sea.

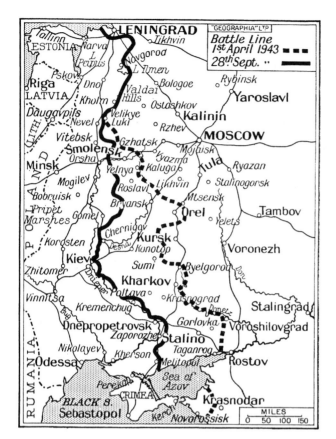

The Eastern Front

Left: A map of the Russian Front showing the territory recaptured from the Germans between 1 April and 28 September 1943. Smolensk had been taken back by the Red Army on 25 September, and by the end of the month the assault would begin on Kiev.

Below: A scene of utter devastation in liberated Smolensk, which had been in German possession for two years, during which time it had been their principal base in the Upper Dnieper region.

Above: German rocket launchers which were used on the Russian Front. The Nebelwerfer (smoke projector) had six barrels or launch chambers and went on to fire a high explosive warhead. The Russians also deployed their own Katyusha rocket banks mounted on trucks. *Below:* The American 'Z' anti-aircraft rockets developed by Dr Alwyn Douglas Crow.

Above: HM Submarine *Tuna*, photographed at Scapa Flow on 29 September 1943. *Below:* French destroyers being salvaged at Toulon in 1943.

OCTOBER 1943

Above: A British Sherman takes the road to Vesuvius. With the capture of Tore Annunziata, the British tanks, loaded with infantry, were detailed to search the streets for enemy snipers.

The Allies entered Naples on 1 October 1943. *Top:* Wrecked and capsized merchant ships litter the harbour, the result of deliberate destruction by the Germans. *Bottom:* Within two hours of the fall of Naples General Mark Clark, Commander-in-Chief 5th Army, arrived to inspect the captured city. *Opposite page:* Damage inflicted by Allied bombers on the marshalling yards in Naples, with a train-load of Luftwaffe aircraft and parts in the foreground.

Above: Wrecked Axis aircraft at Capodichino airfield, near Naples. The remains of an Italian Macchi C200 fighter are in the foreground, with a larger transport aircraft behind. *Below:* The inhabitants of Amalfi take an interest in British anti-aircraft guns which have drawn up in the square. The stone steps lead up to the city's Cathedral of Sant Andrea.

Top left: Clearing a snipers' nest in one of the narrow streets of Campochiaro. This Canadian soldier is using a Mills bomb for the job. *Top right:* Further street fighting in Campochiaro as troops of the 8th Army advance cautiously in the knowledge that there are snipers ahead. *Bottom:* An American bulldozer makes light work of towing a vehicle and mobile gun across the fast-flowing Biferno River near Colle d'Anchise.

Above: British engineers of the 5th Army transporting Bren Carriers across the Volturno on a shore-landing deck-craft. This is being hauled across by hand. *Below:* Once bridgeheads were established on the north bank of the river the engineers constructed pontoon bridges, over which tanks, vehicles and troops could pass in a steady stream.

US Navy Action

Above: A Kingfisher aircraft is being lifted from the sea by crane, in preparation for its next catapult launch from a US battleship. *Below:* Manning the Bofors guns on a battleship. This unit is serving with the British Home Fleet during an exercise of British and US warships.

Above: Loading a Typhoon fighter-bomber with one of two 500-lb bombs. Fitted with four cannon or twelve machine guns, this dual-purpose aircraft proved to be highly effective as a bomber and as a formidable fighter.

The Hawker Typhoon Fighter-Bomber
Above: Three of the latest Hawker Typhoons flying in formation. The British-built aircraft was a single-seat low-wing monoplane of metal construction powered with a Napier-Sabre engine. In its role as a fast bomber the Typhoon participated in daylight raids on railways and airfields in German-occupied territories, as well as attacking shipping and other targets.

Above: A Bristol Beaufighter armed with a torpedo. Operating with Coastal Command these two-man aircraft were deployed to attack enemy shipping. In addition to the torpedo, they were armed with four cannon which are visible as the oval openings on the underside of the nose.

NOVEMBER 1943

Above: An American soldier gives a Chinese comrade a light for his cigarette during a lull in the fighting in Burma.

1943 – The Year of Conferences

Above: Another conference but with a change in line-up. At the Cairo conference, held in November, President Roosevelt and Winston Churchill were joined by China's Chiang Kai-shek, seated on the left. (His interpreter sits next to Churchill). *Below:* This newspaper cartoon depicts the three leaders preparing to deal with 'Japan's Ill-gotten Gains'.

Top left: President F. D. Roosevelt represented the USA at the three conferences. *Top right:* Churchill was at the Teheran and Cairo meetings. *Below left:* The Soviet leader Josef Stalin attended in Teheran. *Below right:* Chiang Kai-shek represented China at the Cairo conference.

Progress for the Allies in Italy
Above: British armoured cars near Rocccaminfina, a village north-east of Sessa Aurunca which was occupied by the 5th Army on 5 November. *Below:* A map with battle line at 23 November.

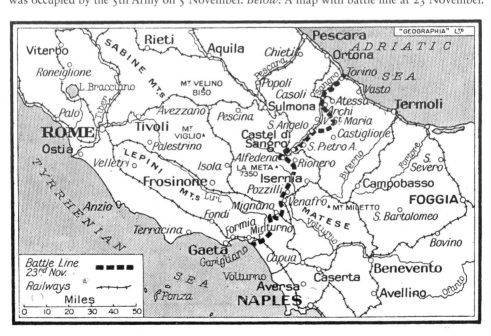

North Africa became an important base for Allied aircraft attacking targets in Italy, Greece and throughout the Mediterranean. *Above:* These Royal Australian Air Force Halifaxes are about to set out on a raid. *Below:* The Luftwaffe also remained active in Italy. Here the sky above Naples is streaked with the lights of anti-aircraft fire and flares dropped by the bombers.

On the lookout for hostile aircraft. *Above:* During the Tunisian campaign these RAF Kittyhawks and Warhawks of the Desert Air Force had provided support for the front-line infantry, and they continued to carry out missions in the region, in particular to maintain a watch for enemy aircraft activity. *Below:* On the Adriatic coast these gunners of the 8th Army are manning a Bofors gun at Termoli, ready to deal with incoming aircraft.

It wasn't always about weapons. *Above:* A shipment of nearly 500 tons of seed potatoes is being unloaded in the dock at Algiers. The seed will be distributed to growers in the region.

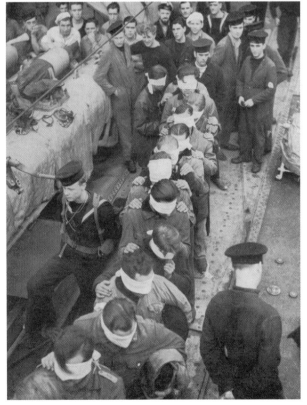

Above: The SS *Vienna* at Ardossan harbour, Scotland, in November 1943. This LNER ship was one of the many railway ferries taken up for wartime service by the Royal Navy.

Left: These survivors of a U-boat sunk by Coastal Command aircraft were picked up by a British destroyer. Blindfolded, they are being walked towards the gangway to disembark for their journey to a prisoner-of-war camp.

DECEMBER 1943

Above: In Italy a young soldier has surrendered to the 8th Army. He is being searched by a New Zealand military policeman.

Above: British soldiers of the 5th Army take cover among the rocks as they move forward in the Monte Camino area. *Below:* Armed with an automatic gun captured from the enemy, this British soldier uses the natural protection of the rocks on the slope of Monte Camino to keep a watch on the German positions.

Above: An American half-track steadily ploughing its way through the thick mud in the Vanafro area, south-east of Monte Marrone. The American troops are with the 5th Army. *Below:* A view of an M7 Priest, with its distinctive 'pulpit' gun ring. This had been supporting the British infantry on the heights of Monte Marrone, on ground dominating the Colti to Arina road.

Above: A Bren Carrier manned by Indian troops. The Sikh soldiers go into battle wearing their customary headdress. *Below:* The ruins of Castel Di Sangro, a scene of utter devastation encountered time after time by the Allied forces as they advanced northwards through Italy.

Above: A group of German prisoners taken in the fighting on the Moro River being taken to a compound. *Below:* A group of sappers enthusiastically greet their Commander-in-Chief, who addressed them from his car to congratulate them on completing a new bridge in record time.

In Russia

Above: German soldiers take cover in the ruins of a building near the battle-front. *Below:* From a slit trench this heavy machine gun unit watches for any sign of Red Army troops.

Above: The Soviet TB-7 four-engined bomber, which is said to have had a range of 3,000 miles. *Below:* As Canada was sharing its war production with both Britain and Russia, these Canadian-built heavy guns are being loaded aboard a ship that will be sailing to Russia.

Above: A night scene at a Mosquito squadron station. The crews stand by their aircraft, discussing the plans for the operation by moonlight.

The RAF in the Azores

The granting of aircraft facilities in the Azores by Portugal enabled the RAF to better position its aircraft to protect Atlantic merchant shipping. *Above:* Landing the first Flying Fortress in the Azores. *Below:* The RAF officers in command of the Azores operation, on the bridge of the ship that took them to Terceira, one of the central islands.

Above: Batterie Todt, one of the major fortifications on the Atlantikwall, located near Cape Gris on the Pas de Calais. Originally with four casements, or *blockhauses*, one is now a museum.

Fortress Europe – Building the Atlantikwall

The Allied landings in Sicily and southern Italy in 1943 served to heighten Hitler's concern that the next 'invasion' was likely be in northern France. Indeed, before the year was out the Allies had appointed General Eisenhower to oversee what would become Operation Overlord, the biggest seaborne landings the world had ever seen, with a provisional date set for May 1945. (As seen earlier, new vehicles and equipment, such as the DUKWs, had been tested on the beaches of Sicily and Italy.) For the Germans work was already well in hand to turn the entire western coast of occupied European mainland into a giant fortification, the imposingly named Atlantikwall. But this was a misnomer as there was no continuous wall, only a series of fortifications and obstacles.

Work on the Atlantikwall, excluding the Channel Island defences, had commenced in the spring of 1942. The Wall extends from the Bay of Biscay in the south to the North Cape, Norway, in the north and covers about 1,700 miles. It was built by the Organisation Todt (OT), the Reich's civil engineering organisation which was named after its founder, Fritz Todt, who had made his reputation with the pre-war construction of Germany's autobahn network. In February 1942 Todt was succeeded by Albert Speer – Hitler's architect and Reich Minister of Armaments and War Production – following his death in a flying accident. Although not a military organisation as such, the work of the OT literally underpinned the Nazis' stranglehold on the occupied territories. Not only through the building of the autobahns, fortifications, V-weapon sites, submarine pens and so on, but also through the controversial use of enforced labour. At the time German propaganda sources suggested that the number of men employed in the Wall's construction was up to the half-million mark by the autumn of 1942. (Such was the scale of the OT that its personnel numbered around 2 million at its peak.) The same sources claim that 20 million cubic metres of earth were excavated and moved in the twelve-month period from May 1942 to May 1943. It is also stated that it took 17,000 cubic metres of cement per single gun of a super-heavy coastal battery. There were two main types of such batteries: Batterie Todt and Batterie Lindeman, named after the well-known artillery general. Four batteries of the Todt type, complete with living quarters for the personnel, were said to have been completed within ten weeks, the work of 15,000 men with 400 trucks.

Putting aside the distasteful ethics of enforced and even slave labour used by the OT, much of the Atlantikwall has survived, particularly the major batteries and blockhouses. They are remarkable structures with their strong geometrical lines, sliced with slots or apertures, sitting within the coastal landscape like works of abstract sculpture, and while some are slowly sinking into the sea or the sand, unlike the Reich they were built to serve many of these solidly built structures will last a thousand years. The effectiveness of the Atlantikwall in keeping the Allied invasion force at bay was put to the test on D-Day, 6 June 1945. This will be covered in the next edition of *The Second World War in Photographs*.

Below: A gun casement on the Atlantikwall, showing some remnants of the camouflage netting. The construction is crude with the shuttering markings clearly visible.

There isn't even half an engine to spare for unnecessary journeys

.. so 'stay put' this Summer

RAILWAY EXECUTIVE COMMITTEE

10 minutes' P·E·A·C·E –so mine's a Minor!

DE RESZKE MINORS are 'peace-time' cigarettes in a double sense. For they are still made from pre-war stocks of fine tobaccos, carefully selected and stored in large quantities to ensure that the De Reszke standard of quality is maintained. That is one reason why Minors, at 6½d. for 10, are out and out 'the best value on the market'.

Up and doing

You can't think or move quickly if your feet hurt. A bunion can put you out of action as surely as a bullet. You're being fair neither to yourself nor your country if you neglect your feet. Be up and doing and free from pain! Get expert advice from Scholl Foot Service. There is no foot trouble which my trained staff cannot with patience correct.

Advice is free. Treatment painless, restful and inexpensive. Scholl Foot Aids for men, women and children are sold at all the best chemists, shoe-dealers and stores.

FOOTNOTES BY DR. SCHOLL

In the Papers
A selection taken from British wartime newspapers and magazines, a mixture of commercial advertisements mingled with official information notices.

take a bath by all means...

Make a clean job of it; get rid of the grime of duty; protect your skin from attack by aggressive germs; feel fine and fit and fresh again. Take a bath . . . a <u>hot</u> bath . . .

but do take it with

WRIGHT'S

Coal Tar Soap

ONE TABLET — ONE COUPON
7½d. per tablet (purchase tax included)

DON'T TAKE CHANCES WITH GERMS..
Kill 'em with

O·syl

The Safe Antiseptic

BUY THE BIG BOTTLE 1/11½d.

(4 times the 7d. size)
Tax included, U.K. only

MADE BY LYSOL LTD